T0020510

BIGGEST NAMES IN SPORTS
STEPHEN CURRY
BASKETBALL STAR

by Hubert Walker

FOCUS
READERS®
NAVIGATOR

WWW.FOCUSREADERS.COM

Copyright © 2021 by Focus Readers®, Lake Elmo, MN 55042. All rights reserved. No part of this book may be reproduced or utilized in any form or by any means without written permission from the publisher.

Focus Readers is distributed by North Star Editions:
sales@northstareditions.com | 888-417-0195

Produced for Focus Readers by Red Line Editorial.

Photographs ©: Frank Gunn/The Canadian Press/AP Images, cover, 1; Carlos Osorio/AP Images, 4–5; Tony Dejak/AP Images, 7; Kyle Terada/Pool Photo/AP Images, 8; Fred Jewell/AP Images, 10–11; Chuck Burton/AP Images, 13; Paul Sakuma/AP Images, 15; Rich Pedroncelli/AP Images, 16–17; Tony Gutierrez/AP Images, 18; Paul Sancya/AP Images, 21; Paul Bereswill/Getty Images Sport/Getty Images, 22–23; Gregory Shamus/Pool Photo/AP Images, 25; Jeff Chiu/AP Images, 27; Red Line Editorial, 29

Library of Congress Cataloging-in-Publication Data
Names: Walker, Hubert, author.
Title: Stephen Curry : basketball star / by Hubert Walker.
Description: Lake Elmo, MN : Focus Readers, [2021] | Series: Biggest names in sports | Includes index. | Audience: Grades 4-6
Identifiers: LCCN 2020037837 (print) | LCCN 2020037838 (ebook) | ISBN 9781644936993 (hardcover) | ISBN 9781644937358 (paperback) | ISBN 9781644938072 (pdf) | ISBN 9781644937716 (ebook)
Subjects: LCSH: Curry, Stephen, 1988---Juvenile literature. | Basketball players--United States--Biography--Juvenile literature. | African American basketball players--United States--Biography--Juvenile literature.
Classification: LCC GV884.C88 W35 2021 (print) | LCC GV884.C88 (ebook) | DDC 796.323092 [B]--dc23
LC record available at https://lccn.loc.gov/2020037837
LC ebook record available at https://lccn.loc.gov/2020037838

Printed in the United States of America
Mankato, MN
062022

ABOUT THE AUTHOR

Hubert Walker enjoys running, hunting, and going to the dog park with his best pal. He grew up in Georgia but moved to Minnesota in 2018. Overall, he loves his new home, but he's not a fan of the cold winters.

TABLE OF CONTENTS

CHAPTER 1

THREE-TIME CHAMPION

Stephen Curry and the Golden State Warriors were just one win away from a title. They were taking on the Cleveland Cavaliers in the 2018 National Basketball Association (NBA) Finals. The Warriors had won the first three games in the best-of-seven series. Now, in Game 4, they were going for a **sweep**.

Stephen Curry was one of the NBA's top scorers during the 2017–18 season.

Curry dribbled up the court early in the first quarter. Several feet behind the three-point line, he squared up for a long shot. A Cavaliers defender leaped toward him. Curry leaned into the defender, hoping to draw a foul. The referee didn't blow his whistle. But Curry's acrobatic shot sailed through the hoop, hitting nothing but net.

Later in the quarter, Cavs forward LeBron James sent a pass to a teammate. Curry stepped in and stole the ball. Then he sprinted to the other end of the court. But instead of driving toward the basket, he pulled up for a three-pointer. And he drained it.

Because of Curry's elite shooting skills, defenders knew they had to guard him closely.

Just before halftime, Warriors forward Kevin Durant brought the ball across midcourt. He passed to Curry, who was behind the three-point line. LeBron James held his arm high to guard the Warriors superstar. Seconds remained on the clock. Curry put up an off-balance shot.

Curry averaged 27.5 points per game in the 2018 NBA Finals.

Once again, he nailed it. The Warriors led 61–52 at halftime.

In the third quarter, Curry received a pass near the three-point line. A Cleveland defender ran toward him. The defender expected Curry to attempt another shot from downtown. But Curry stepped around the defender. Then he dribbled toward the basket and made an impressive layup.

In the end, the game wasn't even close. Golden State crushed Cleveland by a score of 108–85. Curry led all scorers with 37 points. And he showed why many people consider him one of the greatest shooters of all time.

Many basketball fans thought Curry should have won the Finals Most Valuable Player (MVP) Award. Kevin Durant ended up winning it. But Curry wasn't too concerned about that. After all, he had just won the NBA title for the third time in four years.

CHAPTER 2

SCORING MACHINE

Wardell Stephen Curry II was born on March 14, 1988. People called him by his middle name. Stephen spent his first few months in Akron, Ohio. Akron is just south of Cleveland. Stephen's father, Dell, played in the NBA. He was a member of the Cavaliers when Stephen was born. But Dell got picked up by the Charlotte

Dell Curry (30) played 10 of his 16 NBA seasons with the Charlotte Hornets.

Hornets when Stephen was still a baby. So, the family moved to North Carolina.

Stephen loved basketball as a kid. So did his younger brother, Seth. Dell often brought Stephen and Seth to his practices. The boys were able to play with NBA stars. Both of them developed

FAMILY MATTERS

Stephen's younger brother, Seth, also made it to the NBA. In 2019, the brothers faced each other in the Western **Conference** finals. Stephen and the Warriors faced Seth and the Portland Trail Blazers. Their parents sat in the stands, cheering for both teams. Each parent wore a custom-made shirt. One half was a Warriors jersey, and the other half was a Blazers jersey.

Fans began to learn about Stephen Curry's amazing shooting ability during his time at Davidson College.

a strong **work ethic**. They also learned about basketball by watching the pros.

Stephen was a great shooter in high school. But he got little attention from top colleges. Most **scouts** thought he wasn't big enough. So, he attended a small school called Davidson College.

As a freshman in college, Curry averaged 21.5 points per game. The skinny 18-year-old helped Davidson win the conference title that season. He also notched 122 three-pointers. That was a new National Collegiate Athletic Association (NCAA) record for freshmen.

As a sophomore, Curry increased his scoring average to 25.9 points per game. And in the 2008 NCAA tournament, he led his team all the way to the Elite Eight. Curry also set the NCAA record for most three-pointers in a season. He hit 162.

Curry had another great season during his junior year. He set a school record for most career points. He also led all

Curry (center) poses with his parents after the Warriors picked him in the 2009 NBA Draft.

NCAA players in scoring. By then, Curry believed he was good enough to turn pro. So, he skipped his senior year.

In the 2009 NBA **Draft**, the Golden State Warriors selected him in the first round. Curry had proved the top colleges wrong. He was heading to the NBA.

CHAPTER 3

MAKING A SPLASH

Stephen Curry didn't waste any time showing the NBA what he could do. In 2009–10, during his **rookie** season, he drained 166 three-pointers. That was a rookie record. Curry also scored 30 or more points eight times that season.

The 2011–12 season was a tough one for Curry. He dealt with injuries and didn't

Curry and the Warriors finished just 26–56 during his rookie season in 2009–10.

From left to right, Curry, Draymond Green, and Klay Thompson helped turn the Warriors into contenders.

play much. But he came back strong in 2012–13. The young point guard dazzled fans by scoring 272 three-pointers. That set a new single-season record.

Curry wasn't the only Warriors player who could score from downtown.

Teammate Klay Thompson was nearly as good as Curry. Together, Curry and Thompson became known as the Splash Brothers. Warriors fans loved watching the duo sink long shots. They also loved the fact that Golden State reached the playoffs for the first time in years.

ONE-TWO PUNCH

In 2013–14, Curry led the NBA in three-pointers. Thompson finished second. The Splash Brothers set a record with 484 combined threes. The following season, they finished first and second again. They also topped their old record, with 525 total. In 2015–16, they finished first and second for the third season in a row. This time they sank 678. And in 2016–17, they did it yet again, totaling 592.

By the 2013–14 season, the rest of the NBA was beginning to take notice. Curry played in his first All-Star Game. He also helped Golden State make the playoffs again. The Warriors lost a tough series to the Los Angeles Clippers. But the team was moving in the right direction.

In 2014–15, Curry took his game to another level. He sank 286 three-pointers, breaking his own record. He also won the league's MVP Award. Best of all, Curry led his team to the Finals. He lit up the scoreboard, averaging 26 points per game in the series. Golden State beat Cleveland in six games. Curry was an NBA champion!

Curry's red-hot three-point shooting carried the
Warriors all the way to the 2015 championship.

CHAPTER 4

SHOOTING STAR

Warriors coach Steve Kerr knew that Stephen Curry could shoot with amazing **accuracy** from long range. So, he encouraged Curry to attempt more three-pointers.

During the 2015–16 season, Curry did exactly that. He scored an incredible 402 three-pointers. That shattered his

Following the 2015–16 season, Curry had three of the top four seasons for three-pointers in NBA history.

previous record. Curry won his second MVP Award. And the Warriors finished the regular season with the best record in NBA history.

In the Finals, Golden State had a rematch with Cleveland. Curry helped the Warriors build a 3–1 lead in the series. But the Cavs came back. They beat the Warriors in seven games.

Curry didn't let the heartbreaking loss get him down. In 2016–17, he picked up right where he left off. Curry sank 324 three-pointers that season. He also led the Warriors back to the Finals. Once again, they took on Cleveland. And this time, the Warriors came out on top.

Curry and the Warriors got past LeBron James and the Cavaliers for the 2018 title, just like in 2015 and 2017.

The following season, Golden State reached the Finals for the fourth year in a row. They faced the Cavaliers yet again. Curry and the Warriors made it look easy this time. They swept the Cavs in four games. It was Curry's third championship.

Curry's shooting was as good as ever in 2018–19. He dropped 354 three-pointers that season. He also led his team to its fifth straight Finals. However, the Warriors fell short of a **three-peat**. They lost to the Toronto Raptors in six games.

HELPING HAND

In 2020, the COVID-19 **pandemic** spread around the world. Schools closed to keep people safe. However, many kids relied on receiving meals at their schools. Curry worked with a food bank to give free meals to students in Oakland, California. Curry has also worked with other charities during his career. For example, he gave money to a group that fights malaria. This disease kills more than one million people every year.

With Curry leading the way, Warriors fans had reason to believe the team's future remained bright.

A broken hand forced Curry to miss most of the 2019–20 season. However, he came back strong in 2020–21. That season, Curry led the league in scoring. And in 2021–22, Curry led the Warriors to another NBA title. It was the fourth championship of his incredible career.

STEPHEN CURRY

- Height: 6 feet 3 inches (191 cm)
- Weight: 190 pounds (86 kg)
- Birth date: March 14, 1988
- Birthplace: Akron, Ohio
- High school: Charlotte Christian School (Charlotte, North Carolina)
- College: Davidson College (Davidson, North Carolina) (2006–2009)
- NBA team: Golden State Warriors (2009–)
- Major awards: NBA All-Star (2014–2019, 2021–2022); NBA champion (2015, 2017, 2018, 2022); NBA MVP (2015, 2016); NBA Finals MVP (2022); NBA scoring champion (2016, 2021)

Oakland

San Francisco

Akron

Davidson

Charlotte

FOCUS ON
STEPHEN CURRY

Write your answers on a separate piece of paper.

1. Write a paragraph explaining the main ideas of Chapter 3.

2. Do you think Curry could have scored more three-pointers if Klay Thompson had not been on the team? Why or why not?

3. In which season did Curry score 402 three-pointers?
   - **A.** 2011–12
   - **B.** 2015–16
   - **C.** 2018–19

4. What advantage did Stephen have when he was growing up?
   - **A.** He got to practice with NBA players, including his dad.
   - **B.** He was bigger and stronger than most kids his age.
   - **C.** He knew that he would attend a big-name college.

Answer key on page 32.

GLOSSARY

accuracy
The ability to shoot the ball into the basket.

conference
A group of teams within a league.

draft
A system that allows teams to acquire new players coming into a league.

pandemic
A disease that spreads quickly around the world.

rookie
A professional athlete in his or her first year.

scouts
People who look for talented young players.

sweep
Winning all the games in a series.

three-peat
Winning three championships in a row.

work ethic
The ability to stay focused on a task and finish the job.

TO LEARN MORE

BOOKS

Braun, Eric. *Stephen Curry*. Minneapolis: Lerner Publications, 2017.

Campbell, Dave. *Stephen Curry*. Minneapolis: Abdo Publishing, 2017.

Kelley, K. C. *Golden State Warriors*. Mankato, MN: The Child's World, 2019.

NOTE TO EDUCATORS

Visit **www.focusreaders.com** to find lesson plans, activities, links, and other resources related to this title.

INDEX

Answer Key: 1. Answers will vary; **2.** Answers will vary; **3.** B; **4.** A